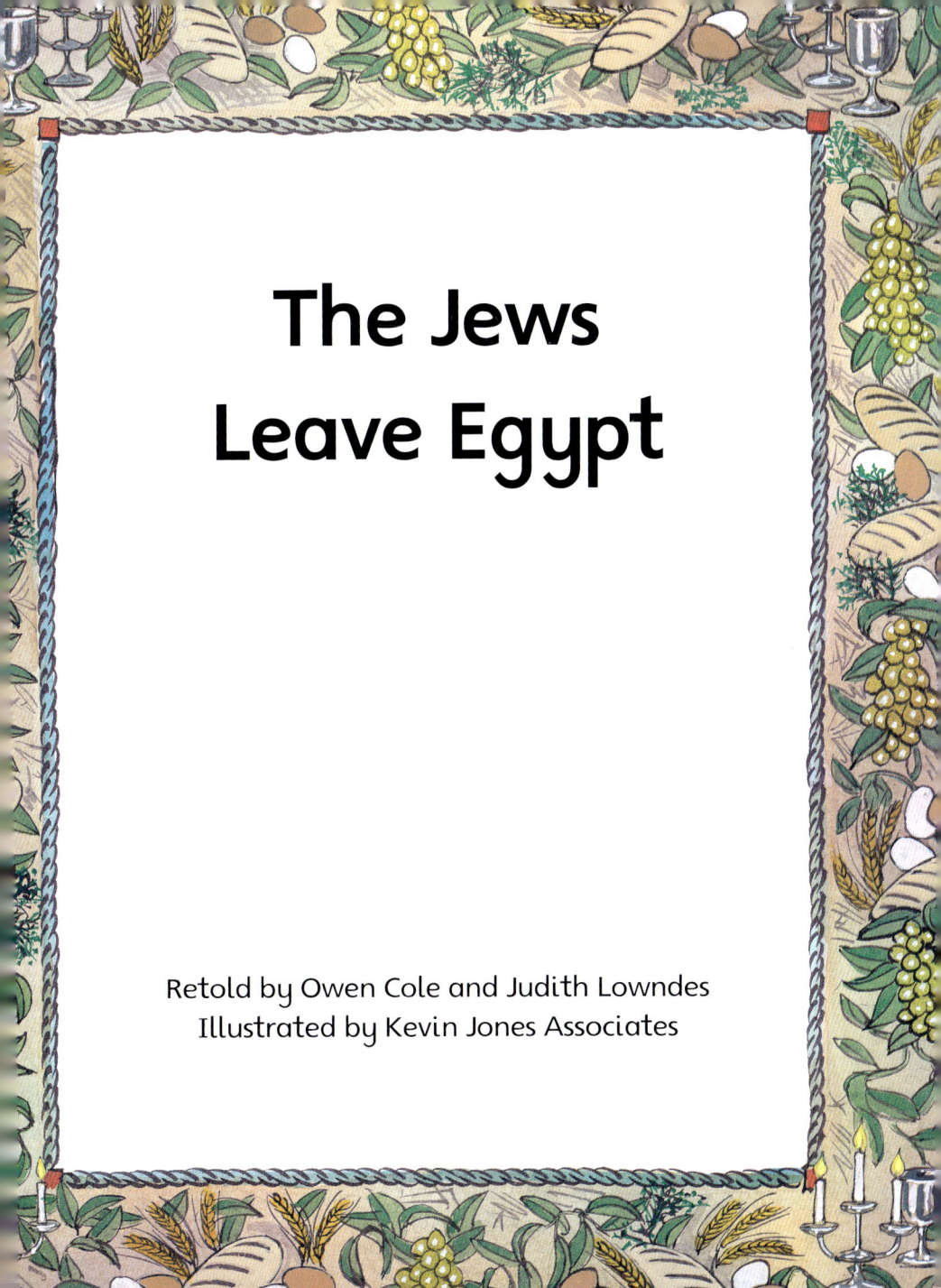

The Jews
Leave Egypt

Retold by Owen Cole and Judith Lowndes
Illustrated by Kevin Jones Associates

Heinemann Educational Publishers
Halley Court, Jordan Hill, Oxford OX2 8EJ

MADRID   ATHENS   PARIS
FLORENCE   PRAGUE   WARSAW
PORTSMOUTH NH   CHICAGO   SAO PAULO
SINGAPORE   TOKYO   MELBOURNE   AUCKLAND
IBADAN   GABORONE   JOHANNESBURG

© Heinemann Educational 1995

First published 1995

95 96 97 98 99 10 9 8 7 6 5 4 3 2 1

British Library Cataloguing in Publication Data
A catalogue record for this book is available from the British Library

Starter Pack
1 of each of 12 titles: ISBN 0 435 01066 2

Library Hardback Edition
The Jews Leave Egypt: ISBN 0 431 07759 2
1 of each of 12 titles: ISBN 0 431 07763 0

Designed by Sue Vaudin; printed and bound in Hong Kong

Acknowledgements
Back cover photograph: Sonia Halliday Photographs

There is a time each year when
Jews have a special meal.
It is called Passover.
They tell a story about God and a
man called Moses.

Moses was a Jew.

He lived many, many years ago.

Moses liked to pray to God.

Moses and the other Jews lived in Egypt.

The king of Egypt was a cruel man.

He did not like the Jews.

He made them work very hard.

He did not let them pray to God.

They were very unhappy.

One day God spoke to Moses.
He said, "Lead the Jews out of Egypt.
They are my people and
I will make them free."

"How can I do that?" said Moses.

"The king of Egypt will not listen to me."

Moses tried to do what God told him.

Moses went to the king of Egypt.

He said to him, "Let the Jews go so that they can worship God."

The cruel king said, "No!"

So God helped the Jews.

God made things happen to all the
people in Egypt.

He made rivers and lakes turn to blood.

Then God made frogs come out of
the river.

They were everywhere, in the ovens and
even in the beds.

Moses went again to the king of Egypt.
He said, "Let the Jews go so that they
can worship God."
But still the king said, "No!"

So God made some more things happen.

He filled the air with gnats and flies.

Then he made the animals in Egypt die.

Then all the people got nasty sores.

Moses went back to the king of Egypt.

He said again, "Let the Jews go."

But the cruel king still said, "No!"

So God made even more things happen.

He made huge hailstones fall.

He made insects eat all the crops.

He made the sky go dark.

Moses spoke again to the king.

The king still said, "No!"

But Moses knew that God was going to

help the Jews leave Egypt.

God told the Jews to put a special
mark over their doors.
God said, "Be ready to leave Egypt."

One night many people died.
But all the Jews who had marks over
their doors were safe.

The people of Egypt were scared.

"Get out of Egypt!" they shouted at
the Jews.

"If you stay we will all die!"

The king of Egypt sent for Moses.

"Get out of Egypt!" he shouted.

"Take your people with you!

Go and worship your God!"

God showed Moses and the Jews the
way to go.
At night time a pillar of fire led them.
In the day a pillar of smoke led them.

God led them across the desert to
the edge of the sea.
But the cruel king of Egypt sent
his army to chase the Jews.

"What shall we do?" they cried.

"The army will kill us!"

But God helped his people.

He made the sea go back.

The Jews walked to the other side.

The army followed them.

Then the sea came back and
the army was drowned.
The Jews were safe.